Alexander

THE

D0036734

DATE DUE

HIGHSMITH #45115

Also by Elizabeth Alexander

POETRY
Body of Life
Antebellum Dream Book

PROSE
The Black Interior

The

Venus Hottentot

ELIZABETH ALEXANDER

Graywolf Press
SAINT PAUL, MINNESOTA

Copyright © 1990 by the Rector and Visitors
of the University of Virginia

First published in 1990 by the University Press of Virginia

Publication of this volume is made possible in part by a grant provided
by the Minnesota State Arts Board, through an appropriation by the
Minnesota State Legislature; a grant from the Wells Fargo Foundation
Minnesota; and a grant from the National Endowment for the Arts.
Significant support has also been provided by the Bush Foundation;
Target, Marshall Field's and Mervyn's with support from the Target
Foundation; the McKnight Foundation; and other generous contributions
from foundations, corporations, and individuals. To these organizations
and individuals we offer our heartfelt thanks.

MINNESOTA
STATE ARTS BOARD

NATIONAL
ENDOWMENT
FOR THE ARTS

Published by Graywolf Press
2402 University Avenue, Suite 203
Saint Paul, Minnesota 55114
All rights reserved.

www.graywolfpress.org

Published in the United States of America

ISBN 978-1-55597-392-6

2 4 6 8 9 7 5 3

Library of Congress Control Number: 2003109139

Cover design: Julie Metz

Cover painting: Carrie Mae Weems, *The Apple of Adam's Eye,* 1993
Courtesy of the artist and PPOW, NY

To my parents,
Clifford and Adele Alexander,
and to my teacher,
Derek Walcott:
this first book,
in gratitude and love

Contents

I

The Venus Hottentot   5

II

West Indian Primer   13
Ode   14
Ladders   15
Zodiac   16
The Dirt-Eaters   17
Who I Think You Are   20
House Party Sonnet: '66   21
Nineteen   22

III

Omni — Albert Murray   25
Robeson at Rutgers   30
Van Der Zee   31
Bearden   33
Deadwood Dick   34
John Col   35
Painting   37
Monet at Giverny   38
Farewell to You   39

IV

Penmanship	43
Letter: Blues	44
Boston Year	46
Kevin of the N.E. Crew	47
Four Bongos: Take a Train	48
"Radio Days"	49
Miami Footnote	50
"Ala	51
A Poem for Nelson Mandela	52
Today's News	54
Preliminary Sketches: Philadelphia	55

THE VENUS HOTTENTOT

I

The Venus Hottentot

(1825)

1. CUVIER

Science, science, science!
Everything is beautiful

blown up beneath my glass.
Colors dazzle insect wings.

A drop of water swirls
like marble. Ordinary

crumbs become stalactites
set in perfect angles

of geometry I'd thought
impossible. Few will

ever see what I see
through this microscope.

Cranial measurements
crowd my notebook pages,

and I am moving closer,
close to how these numbers

signify aspects of
national character.

Her genitalia
will float inside a labeled

pickling jar in the Musée
de l'Homme on a shelf

above Broca's brain:
"the Venus Hottentot."

Elegant facts await me.
Small things in this world are mine.

2.

There is unexpected sun today
in London, and the clouds that
most days sift into this cage
where I am working have dispersed.
I am a black cutout against
a captive blue sky, pivoting
nude so the paying audience
can view my naked buttocks.

I am called "Venus Hottentot."
I left Capetown with a promise
of revenue: half the profits
and my passage home: A boon!
Master's brother proposed the trip;
the magistrate granted me leave.

I would return to my family
a duchess, with watered-silk

dresses and money to grow food,
rouge and powders in glass pots,
silver scissors, a lorgnette,
voile and tulle instead of flax,
cerulean blue instead
of indigo. My brother would
devour sugar-studded non-
pareils, pale taffy, damask plums.

That was years ago. London's
circuses are florid and filthy,
swarming with cabbage-smelling
citizens who stare and query,
"Is it muscle? Bone? Or fat?"
My neighbor to the left is
The Sapient Pig, "The Only
Scholar of His Race." He plays

at cards, tells time and fortunes
by scraping his hooves. Behind
me is Prince Kar-mi, who arches
like a rubber tree and stares back
at the crowd from under the crook
of his knee. A professional
animal trainer shouts my cues.
There are singing mice here.

"The Ball of Duchess DuBarry":
In the engraving I lurch
toward the *belles dames,* mad-eyed, and
they swoon. Men in capes and pince-nez
shield them. Tassels dance at my hips.
In this newspaper lithograph
my buttocks are shown swollen
and luminous as a planet.

Monsieur Cuvier investigates
between my legs, poking, prodding,
sure of his hypothesis.
I half expect him to pull silk
scarves from inside me, paper poppies,
then a rabbit! He complains
at my scent and does not think
I comprehend, but I speak

English. I speak Dutch. I speak
a little French as well, and
languages Monsieur Cuvier
will never know have names.
Now I am bitter and now
I am sick. I eat brown bread,
drink rancid broth. I miss good sun,
miss Mother's *sadza.* My stomach

is frequently queasy from mutton
chops, pale potatoes, blood sausage.
I was certain that this would be
better than farm life. I am
the family entrepreneur!
But there are hours in every day
to conjure my imaginary
daughters, in banana skirts

and ostrich-feather fans.
Since my own genitals are public
I have made other parts private.
In my silence I possess
mouth, larynx, brain, in a single
gesture. I rub my hair
with lanolin, and pose in profile
like a painted Nubian

archer, imagining gold leaf
woven through my hair, and diamonds.
Observe the wordless Odalisque.
I have not forgotten my Khoisan
clicks. My flexible tongue
and healthy mouth bewilder
this man with his rotting teeth.
If he were to let me rise up

from this table, I'd spirit
his knives and cut out his black heart,
seal it with science fluid inside
a bell jar, place it on a low
shelf in a white man's museum
so the whole world could see
it was shriveled and hard,
geometric, deformed, unnatural.

II

West Indian Primer

for Clifford L. Alexander, Sr.
1898–1989

"On the road between Spanish Town
and Kingston," my grandfather said,
"I was born." His father a merchant,
Jewish, from Italy or Spain.

In the great earthquake the ground split
clean, and great-grandfather fell
in the fault with his goat. I don't know
how I got this tale and do not ask.

His black mother taught my grand-
father figures, fixed codfish cakes
and fried plantains, drilled cleanliness,
telling the truth, punctuality.

"There is no man more honest,"
my father says. Years later
I read that Jews passed through my
grandfather's birthplace frequently.

I know more about Toussaint
and Hispaniola than my own
Jamaica and my family tales.
I finger the stories like genie

lamps. I write the West Indian primer.

Ode

The sky was a street map with stars for
house parties, where blue-lit basements
were fever-dreams of the closest a boy
could get to home after yucca fritters,
rice, pigeon peas, and infinite chicken
made by anyone's mother before the night's
charioteer arrived in his beat-up boat
to spirit the three, or the four, or the five, or
as many would fit in the car to the party.
Pennies and pennies bought one red bottle
of Mad Dog Double-Twenty or Boone's Farm.
"Que Pasa, y'all, que pasa," Mister James
Brown sweated, and the Chi-Lites whispered pink.
White Catholic school girls never would dance
or grind or neck or lift their skirts to these
black boys with mothers who spoke little
English and guarded their young with candles
for *los santos,* housework, triple-locked
doors, jars of tinted water, fierce arm-pinches.
Love is a platter of *platanos.*
"Did you hear? Did you hear?"—the young men whisper,
but church calls its altar boys Sunday noon—
"They danced Latin at the Mocambo Room!"
The tale has been told again and again
of boys growing old, going bad, making good,
leaving home while the neighborhood rises
or falls, and this story ends the same.
Now dreadlocked vendors sell mechanized monkeys
programmed to beat *guaguanco.*

Ladders

Filene's department store
near nineteen fifty-three:
An Aunt Jemima floor
display. Red bandanna,

apron holding white rolls
of black fat fast against
the bubbling pancakes, bowls
and bowls of pale batter.

This is what Donna sees
across the "Cookwares" floor,
and hears "Donessa?" *Please,*
this can not be my aunt.

Father's long-gone sister,
nineteen fifty-three. "Girl?"
Had they lost her, missed her?
This is not the question.

This must not be my aunt.
Jemima? Pays the rent.
Family mirrors haunt
their own reflections.

Ladders. Sisters. Nieces.
As soon a live Jemima
as a buck-eyed rhesus
monkey. Girl? Answer me.

Zodiac

You kissed me once and now I wait for more.
We're standing underneath a swollen tree.
A bridge troll waits to snatch me if I cross.
Your bicycle handles are rusted blue.

My mouth has lost its flavor from this kiss.
I taste of warm apple. My lips are fat.
If these blossoms fall they'll mark our faces:
Gold shards of pollen or flower-shaped dents.

Is it bird wings that bat between my legs?
Is there a myth for trolls? Bulfinch says no.
My mother has a friend who reads the stars.
I am fourteen. "My dear, you look in love."

Your fingers stained dull orange from the bike.
Svetlana eyes and hands, no crystal ball.
White ripe blossoms on a trembling tree.
Again, I think. *I want you to kiss me.*

The Dirt-Eaters

Southern Tradition of Eating Dirt Shows
Signs of Waning

   —headline, The New York Times, 2/14/84

tra
dition
wanes
I read
from North
ern South:
D.C.

Never ate
dirt
but I lay
on Great-
grandma's
grave
when I
was small.

"Most cultures
have passed
through
a phase
of earth-
eating
most pre
valent today
among

rural
Southern
black
women."

Geo
phagy:
the practice
of eating
earthy matter
esp. clay
or chalk.

(Shoe-
boxed dirt
shipped North
to kin)

The gos
sips said
that my great-
grand
ma got real
pale when she
was preg
nant:

"Musta ate
chalk,
Musta ate

starch, cuz
why else
did her
babies
look
so white?"

The Ex
pert: "In ano
ther gener
ation I
sus
pect it will dis
appear al
together."

Miss Fannie Glass
of Creuger, Miss.:
"I wish
I had
some dirt
right now."

Her smile
famili
ar as the
smell
of
dirt.

Who I Think You Are

Empty out your pockets nighttime, Daddy.
Keys and pennies, pocket watch, a favored
photograph of Ma, and orange-flavored
sucker-candies, in the dresser caddy.

Grandpa leaves his silver in his trousers,
potions for catarrh set on the bureau,
and his Castile soap. "All Pure." Oh,
those oval, olive cakes for early rousers!

Baba's home is different from my daddy's:
the sofa arms are draped with quiet lace.
Does he fix fish with cardamon and mace?
Coupons in a cookie tin. Meat patties,

Steaming Cream of Wheat and ripe banana,
juice cups with the little paper hats,
the guava jelly jars on plastic mats.
We are your children and receive your manna.

I see you both. I see what's in your pockets.
Coins from you, Dad'. Baba? What's for me?
Fortune cookies, child, and sacks of tea,
cigar bands and glinting, dimestore lockets.

House Party Sonnet: '66

Small, still. Fit through the bannister slit.
Where did our love go? Where did our love go?
Scattered high heels and the carpet rolled back.
Where did our love go? Where did our love go?
My brother and I, tipping down from upstairs
Under the cover of "Where Did Our Love Go?"
Cat-eyed Supremes wearing siren-green gowns.
Pink curls of laughter and hips when they shake
Shake a tambourine *where did our love go?*
Where did our love go? Where did our love go?
Stale chips next morning, shoes under the couch,
Smoke-smelling draperies, water-paled Scotch.
Matches, stray earrings to find and to keep—
Hum of invisible dancers asleep.

Nineteen

That summer in Culpeper, all there was to eat was white:
cauliflower, flounder, white sauce, white ice cream.
I snuck around with an older man who didn't tell me
he was married. I was the baby, drinking rum and Coke
while the men smoked reefer they'd stolen from the
    campers.
I tiptoed with my lover to poison-ivied fields, camp vans.
I never slept. Each fortnight I returned to the city,
black and dusty, with a garbage bag of dirty clothes.

At nineteen it was my first summer away from home.
His beard smelled musty. His eyes were black. "The
    ladies love my hair,"
he'd say, and like a fool I'd smile. He knew everything
about marijuana, how dry it had to be to burn,
how to crush it, sniff it, how to pick the seeds out. He
    said
he learned it all in Vietnam. He brought his son to visit
after one of his days off. I never imagined a mother.
"Can I steal a kiss?" he said, the first thick night in the field.

I asked and asked about Vietnam, how each scar felt,
what combat was like, how the jungle smelled. He listened
to a lot of Marvin Gaye, was all he said, and grabbed
between my legs. I'd creep to my cot before morning.
I'd eat that white food. This was before I understood
that nothing could be ruined in one stroke. A sudden
storm came hard one night; he bolted up inside the van.
"The rain sounded just like that," he said, "on the roofs
    there."

III

Omni—Albert Murray

I. OVERTURE

> *Obviously there is much to be said for the conscious*
> *cultivation and extension of taste, but there is also*
> *something to be said for the functional reaction*
> *to artistic design (and honeysuckles) as normal*
> *elements of human existence.*
>
> —Albert Murray

(three four)   The ancestors are humming: *Write a poem,*
   girl.
Turn up the volume, they say. Loud-talking. Talking loud.
On piano someone plays a boogie-woogie run:
Omni—Albert Murray   Omni Omni   Albert Murray.

In my mind and in his I think a painting is a poem.
A tambourine's a hip shake and train whistle a guitar.
Trains run North/South home their whistles howling
   Afro. . . . Am.
Black and blue   Blue   Afro-blue blue-black and
   blue blew blew.

I can picture Bearden with his magazines and scissors.
I can see guitar shapes, curves like watermelon rinds.
Will I find names like Trueblood and the shapes for my
   collage?
Omni—Albert Murray   Omni Omni   Albert Murray.

2. ELLINGTONIA

So much goes on in a Harlem airshaft. You hear
fights, you smell dinner, you hear people making
love. . . . You see your neighbor's laundry. You hear
the janitor's dogs. . . . One guy is cooking dried
fish and rice and another guy's got a great big
turkey. . . . Jitterbugs are jumping up and down
always over you, never below you.

—Duke Ellington

I might have jitterbugged at the Renaissance 'room,
thrown upside down by some zoot-suited don
in a vicuña coat, smell of Barbasol—
I might have been a barfly with her wig turned 'round.

I conjure smoke-blue clubs from family tales,
names, like "Do Nothing 'til You Hear from Me."
Duke's square-toed leather shoes, his droop-lid eyes,
his—This is a black and tan fantasy.

Not shoes, not conjure, shaving cream, cologne.
"Tootie for Cootie" unafraid of rhyme.
Bold music, bold as sunflowers. Rhyme is real.
Blow smoke rings when you say "Mood Indigo."

3. INTERLUDE

Albert Murray do they call you Al
or Bert or Murray or "Tuskegee Boy"?
Who are the Omni-ones who help me feel?
I'm born after so much. Nostalgia hurts.

4. STELLA BY STARLIGHT

*(after the tune, played by Monty Alexander on
piano and Othello Molyneaux on steel drum)*

Red hair in summertime,
ashy toes, dust-knuckled,
the slim curve of autumn
in sight. In summertime
rhiney, shedding burnt skin,
petticoats, pantaloons.
I'm a rusty-butt sun-
baby, summer is gone.

No more corn and no blue-
berries. Sweet tomatoes
overripe. No more ice
blocks with *tamarindo,*
sweaty love in damp white
sheets, sunflowers, poppies,
salt in summertime,
sun-stoked bones. Summer jones.

Starlight cool as the edge
of fall. "Stella by Star-
light" steals stars for letters.
Each *l* and each *t* pricks
the sky like a star or
a steel drum quiver on
a note 'til it shimmer.
Who is Stella? Summer's

5. BEARDEN AT WORK

> *Regardless of how good you might be at whatever*
> *else you did, you also had to get with the music.*

—Romare Bearden

Paper-cutting rhythm, snips of blue foil
falling onto water-colored paper,
colored people into place. Eye divines
arrangement, hands slide shifting paper shapes.
Panes of color learned from stained-glass windows,
pauses   spacing   rests   from Fatha Hines.

Odysseus is blue. He can't get home.
In Bearden's planes: collage on board, shellac.
Watch Dorothy, children, enter Oz.
Look, Daddy, color! No more white and black.
This is the year of the color TV.
Odysseus is blue and now is black.

New York City at Christmastime. Christmas
tree—shapes like Bearden in Bearden blue.
Tin stars falling on a yellow paper
trumpet. Blue sucked in, blues blown back out.
Black folks on ice skates shine like Christmas trees.
New York glitters like a new idea.

6. CODA

Omni: having unrestricted, universal range.
Coda: a concluding passage, well-proportioned clause.
On piano someone plays a boogie-woogie run:
Omni—Albert Murray   Omni Omni   Albert Murray.

Robeson at Rutgers

Hard to picture, but these Goliath trees
are taller still than Robeson. Outside
vast plate windows in this lecture hall,
I imagine him running down autumn fields,
see his black thighs pumping that machinery
across chalk-painted lines.

                      He loved the woman
in the lab, Eslanda, who saw order
in swimming circles on inch-wide slides, who
made photographs. I picture her standing
in darkness, led by red light, bathing paper
in broth, extracting images. Did this woman smile
to watch white paper darken, to pull wet
from the chemicals Paul Robeson's totem face?

Van Der Zee

(1886-1983)

I say your name: James Van Der Zee
for dancing girls and barbershops
when names were names. That was a time.

From Dutch your name is "by the sea."
A boy in endless Lenox snow
you're open-eyed, lean as the trees.

Waiter and elevator jobs.
Your cigar fingers, rolled-up sleeves,
the sent-away-for photo kit:

Those brownstone textures, marcelled hair,
iron faces, gathered drapery,
smooth foreheads, porcelain basins,

hoary beards, brocaded chairs.
Brown knees and calves in smooth nylons,
straw flower baskets, blacksmith's flames.

Father Divine or Daddy Grace
the blind will see   the lame will walk
Garvey's white plumes and epaulets.

Big Jack Johnson. Bojangles.
Sunshine Sammy. Harlem "Y. M."
Somebody's boy scout son salutes,

a brownskin time-steps. Funerals,
babies. The New York Black Yankees.
"Hey! It's the picture-takin' man!"

Signed "JAMES VANDERZEE N.Y.C."
Black stories in brown photographs—
You're drinking ginger ale and Scotch.

Bearden

One eye is larger than her two black hands.
Sunday hats. Brass trumpets. Flowered dresses.
A woman's holler. River or guitar.

Gigantic ham-hands. Open, singing mouths.
Brown purple mouths, huge hands, and wet-bean eyes.
These opaque eyes are looking straight at you.
Women's haunches. The black backs of skulls.

Black spaces sucking in a breath, like jazz.
Low moons. Women taking tin-tub baths.

Deadwood Dick

Come on and slant your eyes again,
O Buffalo Bill.

—Carl Sandburg

Colored cowboy named Nat Love,
They called him Deadwood Dick.
A black thatch of snakes for hair,
Close-mouthed. Bullet-hipped.

One knee bent like his rifle butt,
Just so. Rope. Saddle. Fringe.
Knock this white boy off my shoulder.
Stone-jawed, cheekboned man.

Mama, there are black cowboys.
A fistful of black crotch.
Deadwood Dick: Don't fuck with me.
Black cowboy. Leather hat.

John Col

I reach from pain to music
great enough to bring me back
                              —Michael S. Harper

trane's horn had words in it
                              —A. B. Spellman

John Col-
trane's "Central Park
West" from the first
the point where

this is not enough
untested pain
imagined shred-
ding of my heart

this poem snipped
from paper   Or
a battered brass
blood-blowing horn

the bloody foot-
lights cup the dark
where red and black
are beautiful

a terrible beau-
ty a terrible
beauty a terrible
beauty a horn

And this brass heart-
beat this red
sob   this   this
John Coltrane Col-
trane song

Monet at Giverny

Iris and haystack. Japanese footbridge.
Knobby poplars, vertical and blue
Or yellow. Floating blossoms of pink light.
Water lilies bloom and bloom and bloom.

There are no frogs. There is no princess here.
Planes of edgeless violet, scraps of light.
Blurred green flames and fingernails of light.
He painted this same pond year after year.

The sky becomes the water, then the deep.
Xanthopsia: Monet saw the light yellow.
Physicians, operations, spectacles—
"Disgusting, I see everything in blue."

Painting

(Frida Kahlo)

I've cropped the black hair Diego loves.
The swatches swarm about my feet.

I've cut a window in my forehead.
See? Diego, skull and bones,

magenta, nighttime fever-dreams.
His walls and walls of scenes of work,

brown women bare, female lilies.
I am spider-eyed among monkeys!

A year in bed   I still see blood
in crimson   olive   orchid   jade.

Look at my heart beat! See my veins!
As I lie bleeding in the street

a woman's sack of gold dust splits:
my bloody body gleaming gold—

I wish I could have painted it!
I will witness my own cremation
because ash is as lovely as fire.

Farewell to You

Each man on this slow train
has Bearden's Brueghel face,
his clean crown, putty-smooth,
eyes wise, no trace

of the colors, shapes behind them,
of paper cut to palms
or rump curves or half-moons,
or rooster-comb.

Through Newark, apple blossoms
line train tracks to the church,
and broken eyes of windows
as these cars lurch

past oil drums, blue and yellow,
like the blues singer's dress,
past empty boxcars stacked
like tenement windows,

or like piano keys
awaiting Fatha Hines,
Willie the Lion Smith.
Sound unwinds,

stanzas float in this notebook
at angles to the page
like the angles of music
in a Bearden clef.

Nausicaa makes jelly:
a green anemone,
snake-hips unmoored
in a blue-black sea.

These stanzas on the page
discarded strips from your collage
salvaged like America:
creole montage.

Honor the artist's vision
of a vast world, black and blue.
Beloved Romare Bearden:
Farewell to you.

IV

Penmanship

I notice older women have better penmanship
than I do. Smooth and even, free from stray hairs,
readable, learned by copying lessons onto
wide-ruled paper in marbleized notebooks, the product
of discipline, of knowing what was expected
and then doing it. I would have done it too, then.

My blue cursive crazes the white letter paper.
"I cannot read you!" friends shriek back, in neater
hand as intimate as pica or block print.
In grade school I painted wild-eyed art class sunsets
with tempera colors absent from nature, finger paints.
One bold boyfriend returned typed letters to sender.

Long before teacher-training school, Grandmother's
        friends
made miles and miles of *m*'s with camel-humps that
grazed the middle, dotted line, humps swelled with plenty
of water to go across deserts and deserts
of vast first halves of alphabets, each uppercase *q*
a perfect, backward *2*. Commas swam off the page.

A favorite teacher's purple curlicues startle
my essays with snarled lines and no Rosetta stone.
I'm trying to neaten up my hand, my open-
classroom, flower-power hand. Am I creeping in
from the margins? Am I now current, legible,
when gold-foil stars are not enough, nor penmanship?

Letter: Blues

Those Great Lake Winds
blow all around:
I'm a light-coat man
in a heavy-coat town.

—Waring Cuney

Yellow freesia arc like twining arms;
I'm buying shower curtains, smoke alarms,
And Washington, and you, Love—states away.
The clouds are flat. The sky is going grey.

I'm fiddling with the juice jug, honey pot,
White chrysanthemums that I just bought.
At home, there is a violet, 3-D moon
And pachysandra vines for me to prune,

And old men with checkered shirts, suspenders,
Paper bags and Cutty bottles, menders
Of frayed things and balding summer lawns,
Watching TV baseball, shelling prawns.

The women that we love! Their slit-eyed ways
Of telling us to mind, pop-eyed dismays.
We need these folks, each one of them. We do.
The insides of my wrists still ache with you.

Does the South watch over wandering ones
Under different moons and different suns?
I have my mother's copper ramekin,
A cigar box to keep your letters in.

At least the swirl ceilings are very high,
And the Super's rummy, sort of sly.
I saw a slate-branched tree sway from the roots—
I've got to buy some proper, winter boots.

So many boxes! Crates and crates of books.
I must get oil soap, bleach, and picture hooks.
A sidewalk crack in Washington, D.C.
Will feed my city dirt roots. Wait for me.

Boston Year

My first week in Cambridge a car full of white boys
tried to run me off the road, and spit through the
    window,
open to ask directions. I was always asking directions
and always driving: to an Armenian market
in Watertown to buy figs and string cheese, apricots,
dark spices and olives from barrels, tubes of paste
with unreadable Arabic labels. I ate
stuffed grape leaves and watched my lips swell in the
    mirror.
The floors of my apartment would never come clean.
Whenever I saw other colored people
in bookshops, or museums, or cafeterias, I'd gasp,
smile shyly, but they'd disappear before I spoke.
What would I have said to them? Come with me? Take
me home? Are you my mother? No. I sat alone
in countless Chinese restaurants eating almond
cookies, sipping tea with spoons and spoons of sugar.
Popcorn and coffee was dinner. When I fainted
from migraine in the grocery store, a Portuguese
man above me mouthed: "No breakfast." He gave me
orange juice and chocolate bars. The color red
sprang into relief singing Wagner's *Walküre*.
Entire tribes gyrated and drummed in my head.
I learned the samba from a Brazilian man
so tiny, so festooned with glitter I was certain
that he slept inside a filigreed, Fabergé egg.
No one at the door: no salesmen, Mormons, meter
readers, exterminators, no Harriet Tubman,
no one. Red notes sounding in a grey trolley town.

Kevin of the N.E. Crew

From the bus I see graffiti:
"Kevin of the N.E. Crew."
These walls cave calls hieroglyphics—
Who am I sit next to you?

Turn your head, boy. Look at me, boy.
Dark day, sweet smell, smoke smell blue.
Split-lip black boy brain smell sweet boy,
Look my way, boy. Look at you.

Nine boys smoking angel weed
Saw a lady that they knew,
Dragged the lady in the alley,
What they do—

Don't look for an explanation
(Broken glass and foot-long pole)
"Baby Love," "Snot-Rag," "Lunchbox," "Chrissie"—
Cave walls heart walls silent hole

Who tongue bled imagination?
Who is know, boy? Who are you?
Hey girl. You girl. Look my way girl.
Look at me girl look at you.

Made them. Claim them. These nine black boys.
Bus stops. Off. Stops. Passing through.
Smoke   glass   cave   walls
    Weed   fence   pole   split
Kevin

Four Bongos: Take a Train

for Vinnie

The drummer wears suspenders to look like
an old-timer, and plays a salsa
"Caravan," bad boy from the panyard with

an evil, evil beat. The conga man
chants Yoruba and shakes his sweat loose on
a girl up front. His hand worries the drum

like a live fish trashing. Call the bassist
"Pops," with his grizzly goatee, his Banshee
yelp, his rhumba step. The hall is fluorescent.

"Take a Train," Lawrence Welk called that tune,
and played. Ellington hovers above this group
like changeable weather, in gabardine.

"Radio Days"

In the movie a Latin bandleader
as a nineteen-forty-four bandleader
cradling a chihuahua. His chanteuse wriggles,
snake-hips in orange and white lily hands.

After the movie, my friend says, "Cugat,"
and I think, "Charo," on a cheap talk show,
her cuchi-cuchi Spanish. Her fingers vanish
into a blue riot of frantic guitar.

The real bandleader is Tito Puente.
The pussy-willow mutt is tired, and mewls.
The frayed orange costume flares out at the bottom;
orange waves break into spume at her feet.

The man sitting behind me, indignant:
"I got radio memories better than that."
"Remember Pearl Harbor?" another friend says.
"I saw Jackie Robinson hit that ball."

Miami Footnote

I could go to any city
and write a poem, so here

I am in Miami, seeing
deco buildings like candy

boxes, peach and mint and seafoam,
dull streets, transvestites,

white bowls of black beans forever.
Someone has named a boulevard

for Arthur Godfrey, and beauty
has a sharp edge everywhere.

In this city at the edge
of America, a perfect ocean

turns to gel around my body.
Is the red light frangipani,

or a neon motel sign?
There is no escaping the warm

water, this pink city, Miami.

for K.H.B., H.S.F., G.A.P.

"Ala

At the hoop you sing "Black man!"
when a teammate scores two points.
I see hear your "Black man!" sing
your "Black man!" and repeat.

There's John Coltrane, sadder still
than Hathaway, both men and black.
I am not a black man. I
am not a black man.   Am not.   I.

Shreveport in Louisiana,
Birmingham in Alabama,
send me listening for your words—
eat them not like grapes but bread.

I am all there is to hold.
I will never love or lose
a father as you did   Love
listen   touch the talking book

All that's left to hold   hear
right ear to the book   I call
your name   your voice   a saxophone
Fingers to the talking book:

bama."   Alabama.   What you said.

A Poem for Nelson Mandela

Here where I live it is Sunday.
From my room I hear black
children playing between houses
and the El at a Sabbath rattle.
I smell barbecue from every direction
and hear black hands tolling church bells,
hear wind hissing through elm trees
through dry grasses

        On a rooftop of a prison
in South Africa Nelson Mandela
tends garden and has a birthday,
as my Jamaican grandfather in Harlem, New York
raises tomatoes and turns ninety-one.
I have taken touch for granted: my grandfather's hands,
his shoulders, his pajamas which smell of vitamin pills.
I have taken a lover's touch for granted,
recall my lover's touch from this morning
as Mandela's wife pulls memories through years
and years

        my life is black and filled with fortune.
Nelson Mandela is with me because I believe
in symbols; symbols bear power; symbols demand
power; and that is how a nation
follows a man who leads from prison
and cannot speak to them. Nelson Mandela
is with me because I am a black girl

who honors her elders, who loves
her grandfather, who is a black daughter
as Mandela's daughters are black
daughters. This is Philadelphia
and I see this Sunday clean.

Today's News

Heavyweight champion of the world Mike Tyson
broke his fist in a street brawl in Harlem
at 3 A.M. outside an all-night clothing store
where he was buying an 800-dollar, white
leather coat. The other dude, on TV, said,
"It was a sucker punch." Muhammad Ali said
Tyson ain't pretty enough to be heavyweight
champion of the world. Years ago a new Ali
threw his Olympic gold into the Ohio
River, said he'd get it when black people were truly
free in this country. In South Africa there is a dance
that says   we are fed up   we have no work   you have
struck a rock. I saw it on today's news.

I didn't want to write a poem that said "blackness
is," because we know better than anyone
that we are not one or ten or ten thousand things
Not one poem   We could count ourselves forever
and never agree on the number. When the first
black Olympic gymnast was black and on TV I called
home to say it was colored on channel three
in nineteen eighty-eight. Most mornings these days
Ralph Edwards comes into the bedroom and says,
    "Elizabeth,
this is your life. Get up and look for color,
look for color everywhere."

Preliminary Sketches: Philadelphia

*I saw a friend from growing up who's been living
in L.A. for about twenty years, and I heard him
say, "I'm from L.A.," and I said, "No, man,
you from Philly. We don't give nobody up."*

—Khan Jamal
jazz vibraphonist

Fish-man comes with trout and fresh crabs:
"Live! They live crabs! They live crabs!"
Bars called "Watutsi." "Pony-Tail."

A dark green suit, a banded hat.
The gentleman buys pig's feet and
papaya juice. He looks like church.

Another man, down Spruce Street, says,
"Yeah, California's beautiful,"
but I ain't got no people there,

so I came back. I raised a racehorse.
Trainer says he's mean, but I say
naw, naw. That horse just alive."

Which way to walk down these tree streets
and find home cooking, boundless love?
Double-dutching on front porches,

men in sleeveless undershirts.
I'm listening for the Philly sound—
Brother   brother   brotherly love.

ELIZABETH ALEXANDER was born in New York City and raised in Washington, D.C. She is the author of four collections of poetry, *The Venus Hottentot, Body of Life, Antebellum Dream Book,* and *American Sublime,* which was a finalist for the 2005 Pulitzer Prize in Poetry. She is also the author of two collections of essays, *The Black Interior* and *Power and Possibility: Essays, Interviews, Reviews,* and a collection of poems for young adults, *Miss Crandall's School for Young Ladies and Little Misses of Color* (co-authored with Marilyn Nelson). She recently edited *The Essential Gwendolyn Brooks.* She has read her work across the United States and in Europe, the Caribbean, and South America, and her poetry, short stories, and critical prose have been published in numerous periodicals and anthologies. On January 20, 2009, Alexander delivered a poem at the inauguration of President Barack Obama. She is the recipient of the Alphonse Fletcher, Sr. Fellowship for work that "contributes to improving race relations in American society and furthers the broad social goals of the U.S. Supreme Court's Brown v. Board of Education decision of 1954," and the 2007 Jackson Prize for Poetry, awarded by Poets and Writers. Alexander is a professor of African American Studies and American Studies at Yale University, and also teaches in the Cave Canem Poetry Workshop. She lives with her family in New Haven, Connecticut.

The Venus Hottentot has been set in Galliard, a typeface designed by Matthew Carter.

Book design by Wendy Holdman.
Composition by BookMobile Design and
   Publishing Services.
Manufactured by Bang Printing on acid-free paper.